HOW TO SAVE
A SMALL BUSINESS

By
Ian Turner

Copyright © 2014 by Ian Turner

All rights reserved. No part of this publication may be reproduced, distributed, or transmitted in any form or by any means, including photocopying, recording, or other electronic or mechanical methods, without the prior written permission of the publisher, except in the case of brief quotations embodied in critical reviews and certain other noncommercial uses permitted by copyright law.

Thanks to the thousands of business owners and entrepreneurs I've met over the years that have shared their fears, passions, problems and successes with me.

And, good look to millions of entrepreneurs and business owners that are willing to risk it all in pursuit of a dream.

About the Author

Ian Turner is both a serial entrepreneur, business coach, author and speaker. Having spent the best part of thirty years involved in solving the problems of small to mid-sized businesses, he's got the insight of a well-honed expert business strategist.

Ian's one-on-one heartfelt approach doesn't mean it's softly softly. It's anything but! It means he understands the pressure people face when they make the decision to go into business for themselves.

What makes Ian Turner different? The business owner's challenges are considered personal challenges. When you've worked with thousands of business owners over the years that are facing catastrophic challenges it has to be personal, according to Ian. Ian Turner's goal is to help small business owners build better, stronger businesses that make a positive impact on everyone involved. Families, employees and communities.

Staying true to his sense of community Ian also helps non-profits.

How To Save A Small Business

Respected by business owners, attorneys and accountants alike for his ability to steer a client through crisis of every kind. Ian still coaches and writes for small business.

Other book titles by Ian Turner

Reputation Management: What a business owner really needs to know

82% of consumers have stopped doing business with a company as a result of a negative experience.

79% of consumers that had a negative experience with a company told others about it.

49% of consumers said they would be willing to go back to a company after a negative experience if they were offered proof of enhanced service.

This is an end-to-end look at the reputation management industry, problems, players and solutions.

This simple to read book provides every business owner with a major short-cut through the valuable learning curve that equals wasted time, money, opportunity and heartache.

How to Make Your Small Business a Big Success

Millions of people worldwide are either thinking about going into business for themselves or they are already in business for themselves. For many different reasons people choose a goal of independence, freedom and possibly the financial rewards of success without first thinking through the many what-if's that can lead to business failure.

If we start thinking about the business of the business we have the power to create the business we want. Most entrepreneurs, and small business owners start thinking and working in the business before they ever figured out the business of the business.

Most small businesses struggle to survive every day and they don't have to. This book is going to help us create an unforgettable roadmap to success.

How To Save A Small Business

You can find more information about Ian Turner at:

www.howtogetsmallbusinesshelp.com

www.facebook.com/author/ianturner

www.facebook.com/pages/How-To-Get-Small-Business-Helpcom

www.amazon.com/author/ianturner

Table of Contents

Preface xi

Section 1 - Introduction 1

Section 2 - Options 6

Turnaround Specialists 6

Bank Referred Specialists 8

Self-Sponsored Turnaround 9

Can I turn things around and save my business?
.... 10

Is turning around my business necessary? 10

Should I sell the business before it goes under? 11

Do I need to file bankruptcy? 13

How do I start? 13

Section 3 - Protect Your Assets 15

Protect yourself and your family first 15

Legal considerations 15

How To Save A Small Business

Two tests for the Zone of Insolvency 16

What's expected, once you are in the "zone"? 17

For businesses in general 17

Navigating the turbulent waters of the "zone" .. 18

The Business Judgment Rule 19

Your responsibilities to investors 21

Your responsibilities to creditors 22

Personal asset protection 23

Pay the 941/940 Employee Portion of the Taxes
.... 24

Pay your 941's or live to regret it 25

Fraudulent conveyance 26

More on Personal asset protection 28

Strategic funding of your business 30

Trusts & Other Entities 32

Insurance 33

Personal Guarantees 34

Marriage and family – you and your spouse should: 35

Emotional health..36

Surviving the crisis: How to get through the next 90 days 37

You must quickly decide the status - quickly 37

IMPORTANT: You must stop writing checks until you have a base to make decisions from. 37

Section 4 - Manage a Crisis...................................38

Surviving the crisis: How to get through the next 90 days 38

Quickly decide the status 39

Are you on track to survive the next six months without taking any action? 39

Take control of cash right now!................................39

Forecast cash 42

How to create the cash forecast 43

Find cost savings..45

Restructure the trade debt 46

Layoff deadwood and underperformers 46

Collect money from your customers 46

Sell the receivables to a factoring company 47

Start restructuring the long-term agreements .. 48

Start restructuring long-term bank debt 50

Sell unproductive assets 50

Look at sales and leaseback 50

Section 5 - Get Back By Design 52

Accelerating the solution, do you need more help? 53

Decide if you need any of the following to help lift the weight off your shoulders: 53

For each expert that you need, do the following 54

Creating a Winning Turnaround Plan 54

Act like a turnaround leader 54

Gather information 55

Analyze the data and create your turnaround strategies 57

Build a new management team 58

Hold an alignment meeting with new management team..58

Write the final turnaround plan and create an action plan 59

Rethinking the organizational structure for success..59

Use the "quick" method for designing your structure..60

Use budgets 61

Having a successful interaction with your banker 61

The layoff..62

Decide on a severance package 62

Select a date and time for the layoff 62

Run the termination meeting professionally......63

How To Save A Small Business

Hold the Remaining Employee meeting 65

How to motivate the remaining employees during the turnaround 66

Reducing your debt! 68

Do-it-yourself debt restructuring 68

Debt restructuring – Using a professional 68

Ways to find more money fast 69

Stay and Grow or Sell 70

Celebrate your turnaround success 70

Conclusion 71

Preface

Millions of people worldwide are struggling to keep their business going. For many different reasons people choose what they think is going to be a life of independence, freedom and financial rewards only to have their dreams crushed.

I take my hat off to everyone with the courage and the desire to forge their own path down a road that leads to the personal achievement of their goals in life. Everyone's definition of success is different. Everyone's reason for being in business for themselves is different. Failure on the other hand seems to look and feel the same for most people.

First let me make it clear that I've helped thousands of small business owners over the years. I've worked with businesses during their birth, infancy, puberty, and adolescence, full of life and close to death. And yes, I've witnessed my fair share of businesses that have died.

The saddest part of a business that dies is knowing that it could have lived. It could have prospered.

How To Save A Small Business

Businesses and their owners go through cycles. Economies fluctuate.

Think about this one thing before you let a business close; if that business doesn't have a majority of the marketplace it serves then it's never the economy that hurts the business.

The good news is that it means the business never learned how to compete, and that's an internal struggle. Even in a bad economy great businesses prosper.

If your business is struggling you need to act quickly. There's no getting back the days that you've lost.

Start by reading this book. Most small businesses struggle to survive every day and they don't have to. This book is going to help you find your way back to success.

How To Save
A Small Business

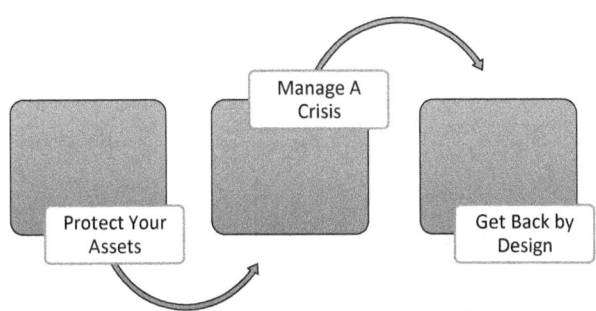

Section 1 – Introduction

When a business is in trouble, the last thing you need is a book full of technical jargon to read, understand, hypothesis, and philosophize over. When you're feeling the most pressure of your life because your family has been seriously hurt in an accident it's not the time to go study for a medical exam. It's time to take action.

The only way to save a business is by realizing a sense of urgency around changes that have to be made. The number one hindrance to saving a business is the business owner themselves. They leave it too late or they want to make minimal changes and then wait to see how it goes. The "*How to Save a Small Business*" isn't about extending the pain of killing a business slowly. When a business is struggling these concerns are real:

- The business is failing.
- The employees, family and friends will be out of jobs.
- You can lose everything you have.
- You may lose your home.
- Your marriage can fail because of the pressure.
- Your vendors and creditors might sue you.
- Making the change to being an employee for someone else may seem impossible.
- Any savings will be gone.
- The damage will last for years.
- You ask yourself was it all for nothing.
- You feel like a failure.

So let's cut all of the fluff and get straight to the point at every stage. The purpose of this book is to give everyone enough of the right information to adapt to a business – to save the business. If you want to learn how to be a turnaround specialist, this isn't the time. I can stack the shelves with turnaround books written for professionals and large corporations, but those books can take months to read and they still don't provide the entrepreneur or small business owner with a clear path to controls and answers. I am going to do everything I can to give you the tools and the motivation to create time and control enough to save a business.

Turning around a business is a daunting task in itself without getting into the academics and science of minutia. Stay focused on the topic, subject and task. Think of this as a process of managing change. This process has been around for years within the turnaround industry and is used on a daily basis by professionals. You are not trying to be perfect, polished or expert. You are trying to save a business.

There is a ton of valuable information available if you care to jump into the science and details of turning around distressed businesses. Experience tells me that an entrepreneur in trouble doesn't need the history of... They need bite size pieces of information they can process and implement – now! Stop the bleeding and deal with the trauma and there is plenty of time for corrective surgeries later.

It's no secret that businesses always have and always will fail. Hundreds of thousands of businesses open and close every single year. The majority of businesses don't last 5 years. Most of the businesses that make it to 10 years are living a life of struggle. Staying open so that the debts and personal guarantees don't get called in, is a common reality for entrepreneurs of small business.

I've yet to see one small business that created 100% of the mess they find themselves in. I've seen as many smart entrepreneurs as I've seen not so smart entrepreneurs struggling in business.

A business isn't guaranteed to fail! You're taking the first step to saving a business. Take a deep breath and stand up tall. You need to be a tower of strength and I'm going to show you how. While everyone can benefit from reading this book, from here on out, it's the entrepreneur and business owner that I'm addressing.

Section 2 - Options

You could hire a turnaround manager, specialist, or consultant by whatever name they choose to call themselves. You could pick from a list of three that your bank may have cleverly persuaded you to choose from. Or you can do it yourself.

Turnaround Specialists

A good specialist is worth their weight in gold and a bad one is going to drag you further down the road. If you are thinking of hiring a specialist you need to get references from entrepreneurs and not from anyone else. You need real references. Ask for a list of ten and choose your own three to call on.

Don't buy the line that "my client list is confidential". BS!

You have no time for BS, you have no time for spending large amounts of time, money and resources with someone that isn't the right fit.

Why do I say fit? Because if someone has a history of saving dental surgeries but you're a baker or a manufacturer, you'll now need to let them learn all about the baking or manufacturing business on your money. Make sure you find someone that already knows the intricacies of your business if you are going to spend tens of thousands of dollars or pounds or whatever your currency is with someone.

A good turnaround specialist can cost well over $250 per hour. From an initial meeting or consultation, you and the specialist will need to determine each other's roles. You'll also need to establish a budget. How many hours a week are you willing to have the specialist involved? On site or off site? Full week or partial week, month to month or six month contract, possibly longer.

I can tell you that saving a business doesn't happen overnight. It takes about 4 months to measurably change a business's direction and twelve months of tweaking, changing and monitoring to make sure the changes are for both short term and long term success.

During the recession, specialists were in high demand and short on supply. What was driving the specialists demand? It sure as heck wasn't the entrepreneurs calling them! It was the banks that had them on speed dial.

Bank Referred Specialists

Your once friendly banker is taking a special interest in getting any moneys lent to you or your business back. It may have nothing to do with you and your business or it may have something. The reasons are irrelevant.

Your bank "strongly suggests" via whatever form they choose to communicate, that you should choose 1 of 3 specialist groups that they refer to you. The referred specialist you choose is going to help you get back on your feet. Get things cleaned up...

I hope your mother told you about Little Red Riding Hood, because your friendly banker is no longer Grandma. Your banker is the Wolf!

Any one of the referred specialists works unofficially for the bank. I don't care what the specialists says to you. The specialist's job is to figure out how to get the bank back its money with no regard for what happens to the entrepreneurs business. Let's call it what it is shall we?

First of all the bank is going to make you feel like you have no choice in the matter or who you choose. You do have a say in the matter. The bank isn't paying for the specialist you are.

Because you feel like you have no choice you pay whatever the specialist suggests. The specialist has already looked at your numbers and they have a good feel for what you can pay if they make certain cuts. That's their bill taken care of, but what about saving your business? Hmm!

Cash flow and assets. What can the specialist cut to create substantial cash flow to the bank, and what's the value of assets when either sold at auction or accounts receivable collected?

The bank referred specialist is going to get his next referral the same way that he got his last referral, from the bank! What makes you think the bank is going to refer this specialist? He managed to get the bank back its money!!!

Now what part of that has anything to do with saving or helping the entrepreneur or the small business? Nothing!

Self-Sponsored Turnaround

Questions you ask yourself:

- Can I turn things around and save my business?
- Is turning around my business necessary?
- Should I sell my business before it goes under?
- Do I need to file bankruptcy?
- How do I start?

Can I turn things around and save my business?

I'm sure you've heard of the miraculous survival stories of people that faced overwhelming odds. The rock climber that fell down a crevasse and had to remove his own arm with a penknife to survive. The sailors that lost at sea should have died but didn't. The people trapped for days underground or under fallen buildings that again survived by beating all of the odds.

What are you capable of, no one knows until you make the decision to give survival everything you've got.

Is turning around my business necessary?

Here's the best part; even the very best of businesses need constant turning around. Or at least the same types of thinking and controls. That's how they become the best businesses. If you're running a healthy business by accident, it's only a matter of time before you're heading for survival mode. In over 15 years, I have only met with one entrepreneur that was in as good as shape as any. I couldn't find issue with anything in his business. His systems and controls, plans and attitudes were fantastic. He doesn't exist today. He was an $80 million a year home builder. I looked at his business years before the housing crash. I have no doubt that he made a deliberate decision to close while he was on the right side of the crash because of how he kept inventory differently than his competitors.

Entrepreneurs should always be looking for what's wrong with their business. This home builder brought me in to find his weaknesses. He had strategies in place to cover everything including an unspoken housing crash!!

Should I sell the business before it goes under?

Try selling a healthy small business before you have ideas of selling an unhealthy small business. The truth is that small businesses are worth more to their owners than they are to anyone else. Can I defend that by filling up 50 pages of why? Yes. But his isn't the time for that argument.

There is an entire industry of Small Business Brokers and self-named "Investment Bankers" that will give the struggling entrepreneur enough hope or even false promises for them to write a check to the professional (sales person) to prepare the business for sale. They'll value the business, prepare an offering of some kind… List a number of really valuable services they will provide to sell your business.

What they don't tell you is that by the industries own definition over 80% of small businesses don't sell!!

Now try selling a struggling small business for more than the auction value of what goes on the auctioneers block!

Contrary to the salesman's line of assurances without making promises that entrepreneurs are being given; buyers are not lining up to pay top price for struggling businesses. Foreign buyers are not using the exchange rate and a visa/passport program to justify buying a failing business.

Do I need to file bankruptcy?

Maybe, maybe not! Bankruptcy is a method of last resort. It's not the first resort. If you ask the majority of bankruptcy attorneys if you should file bankruptcy the answer is yes!

Folks, if you ask most carpet fitters if you need new carpet, most are going to say yes!

Only a few bankruptcy attorneys are going to study your problems and determine if other strategies that are similar to bankruptcy might be more suitable. Pre-bankruptcy strategies might be equally or more valuable to the health and wellbeing of the business and may even open the door to a reduction or restructuring of debt, leases, payables... All without filing bankruptcy.

How do I start?

If you're reading this, you already did start! Every day you wait to do something is reducing your chance to save your business. The faster you move, the fewer problems you have to solve, and the more cash you'll have available.

Section 3 - Protect Your Assets
Protect yourself and your family first
Legal considerations

- Act ethically and legally
- Know when you are in the "zone of insolvency."
- Commit to turning around the business
- Buy a Directors & Officers (D&O) liability policy
- Increase existing (D&O) liability policies as much as possible
- Discuss with your insurance broker the "tail" of the D&O policy
- Commit to staying with the business through its difficulties (important for partners)
- Avoid fraudulent conveyance

- Fix any fraudulent conveyances from the past year
- Get an attorney that understands business law and bankruptcy

Two tests for the Zone of Insolvency

There are really two primary tests for determining insolvency:

1. Balance sheet test: a business is insolvent if its liabilities exceed the fair value of its assets.

2. Cash flow test: a business is insolvent if it is unable to pay its debts as they become due in the ordinary course of business.

In reality, small businesses continually operate within the first definition. And sometimes for years.

That said, each business must take a long look at the facts surrounding their ability to raise additional capital to get them out of this zone. Merely "hoping" that you will raise more money in the short term does not take you out of the Zone of Insolvency…

What's expected, once you are in the "zone"?

If a business is in this Zone of Insolvency, there are certain legal actions which are reasonably expected of the business and its Directors and Officers.

For businesses in general

The directors and officers of an insolvent business have fiduciary duties of care and loyalty to both the creditors and the stockholders.

Basically your creditors are treated as future owners of the business. Therefore you cannot dispel or disburse of any asset in any way that might hurt the so called or treated – future owners. Creditors may bring claims against Directors and Officers for a breach of these duties.

A business attorney should give you advice about what the specific exposure is. There is a theory that if the business knowingly incurs debts after it has recognized that it is in the Zone of Insolvency, the Directors and Officer have allowed a fraud to be committed, and as such, they become personally liable for these debts. This is difficult to prove, but it has been done. In these cases, D&O insurance will not protect the D's and O's because "fraud" is not a covered liability in these policies.

Navigating the turbulent waters of the "zone"

So, what are we supposed to do to avoid liability and abide by the legal requirements of each State of incorporation?

The short answer is get an attorney, the D's & O's are supposed to stop incurring ANY liability after knowingly having entered this Zone of Insolvency. This means, no increased payroll, contract or vendor costs are to be incurred. This could mean furloughing employees, or simply laying them off. It could mean notifying your creditors that you are in the zone, and gaining an agreement to not incur further liability without having a solid plan to leave this zone.

Before you run for the hills you should know that a large number of smaller businesses are always operating in the zone. By following the information in *"How to Save a Small Business"* we want to get you out of the zone. And while in the zone to not knowingly expose yourself to increased liability.

Below are some important things for you to remember as you navigate the Zone of Insolvency:

First thing is to focus internally - Conserve cash—scrub the balance sheet to convert whatever assets are available into liquid resources, like CASH.

Reserve cash for statutory obligations and liquidation costs. Statutory obligations include payroll and payroll taxes.

The Business Judgment Rule

Before receiving recommendations on how to deal with your increased liability, here's some information about the Business Judgment Rule. Fiduciary duties do not require the business owners, CEOs, directors or officers to be perfect or mistake free when running the business. Otherwise, there would be D&O lawsuits every time a business had a slight upset or did not grow as much as some "expert" expected.

This protection from ordinary mistakes is the Business Judgment Rule. Under it, the business leaders are not liable for poor decisions if they have acted in the following ways:

- Without any intent to defraud or deceive
- With enough information
- In the best interests of the investors
- In the best interests of the creditors if the business is insolvent or close to insolvent

Therefore, if you acted as above, the investors and creditors cannot hold you liable for the business getting into trouble. The main concern is to run the business in the best interests of both the investors and the creditors so neither party sues you.

- Buy a Directors & Officers liability policy
- Increase your Directors & Officers liability policy as much as possible
- Ask the insurance broker about the "tail" of the D&O policy

If you are a director, an officer, a CEO or business owner of a troubled business, you need to be especially careful. You now have two groups to whom you must answer: investors and creditors.

As we know, these two groups have conflicting interests. Therefore, if you give advantage to one group over the other, you increase the chances of the offended party suing you. To keep out of trouble, you need to know the responsibilities to each group.

Your responsibilities to investors

You have the responsibility of exercising care in their governance of the business and loyalty to the investors of the business – even if the only investor is your spouse. This is your fiduciary responsibility. Here is what that means:

- You must act in the best interests of *the business and its investors*

- You must act in good faith. You must not have any intent of fraud, deceit or misconduct

- You must decide the business's strategy

- You must replace top management if they have mismanaged the business (for board members of corporate entities)

- You must educate yourself fully about the issues facing the business so you can soundly lead the business

Your responsibilities to creditors

Under normal circumstance, your contracts lay out your only duties to your creditors. This changes when your business enters the zone of insolvency. When you are in the zone of insolvency, you have the following fiduciary responsibilities to creditors:

- You must act in the best interests of the *creditors*

- You must act in good faith. You must not have any intent of fraud, deceit or misconduct

- You must decide the business's strategy

- You must replace top management if they have mismanaged the business (for board members of corporate entities)

- You must educate yourself fully about the issues facing the business so you can soundly lead the business

As you can see by looking at the two sets of fiduciary duties, the responsibilities are the same except you must act in the best interest of *both* investors and creditors. This is a difficult task. Which is why the personal liability increases significantly when the business gets into trouble.

Personal asset protection

- Get an estate planner

- Get a personal asset plan immediately

- Transfer liens and personal guarantees to nonexempt property

- Set up the business as a separate legal entity

- Consider strategic funding of the business (that is move assets legitimately into your name)

- Explore trusts and holding businesses with an estate planner

- Continue to pay the insurance premiums throughout the turnaround

- Keep the business running at least a year for full asset protection

Pay the 941/940 Employee Portion of the Taxes

Whatever you do pay the 941 taxes. You have never met a debt collector like the IRS! 941's will stay with you personally for up to 15 years. Long after everything else is gone you will be paying 941's plus penalties and interest from anywhere the IRS can take it. Think that's not bad enough.

Every company in the world that says they can cut your 941 liability down and make all your problems go away is going to contact you more often than a debt collector. They think you're backed into a corner and the aggressive sales tactics are going to come hard and fast – for months. Your business will be called several times a day and the sales people don't care who they tell about your tax problem.

Still not bad enough! You are going to hire the first company that makes sense, because you're in a corner and you're going to find out after paying them a few thousand dollars that they've done nothing more than make the situation worse. All this time they've been telling you that you are not to talk to the IRS because "the IRS can trick you"! You'll eventually get wise and try again. This time you'll do a little better, but the result will be similar. The tax solution industry is full of scoundrels that are ready and able to take advantage of your plight – and they will!

Pay your 941's or live to regret it

You and the other officers of the corporation are personally liable for the employee-paid portion of their taxes. These are the so-called "trust funds." Make sure that you pay at a minimum this amount of tax to the state and local governments and clearly mark the payment as for the employees. If you don't, be sure the taxing authority will come after your personal bank account for these back taxes.

By the way, you are not personally liable for the company's portion, but only for taxes paid by the employees through you.)

Fraudulent conveyance

A fraudulent conveyance is committed when you give away or sell assets for too little payment. A fraudulent conveyance comes in two flavors. There are fraudulent conveyances with intent and those without intent.

The legal profession calls those without intent "constructive fraudulent conveyances."

Here is an example. Your company will declare bankruptcy soon. Therefore, you decide to give a "present" to your son-in-law. He is a web designer and you allow him to buy your firm's high-end server for a dollar. You just bought it last month for $10,000.

When you've completed this transaction, you have just committed a crime. Effectively, you have stolen from the firm's estate. In addition, you have breached your fiduciary responsibilities to the creditors and investors.

Therefore, by making this gift, you have opened yourself up to a criminal investigation, a creditor lawsuit and an investor lawsuit.

To be clear, this crime will not surface until the bankruptcy court evaluates your business transactions for the past two years (which is the law's "look back" period.) From this review, they will find the fraud. Therefore, if you have sold or given away anything for much below market value in the past two years, you have one of two choices. Either reverse the transaction quickly or refund the difference to the company from your own pocket.

This transaction with your son-in-law would not have been a fraudulent conveyance with intent if you had sold it to him for the market value of a one-month old server. For example, if you sold it to him for $7,500, then likely the court would see this as a reasonable sale. Further, if you could show that they bought the server with the belief the firm was a "going concern," this would increase the transaction's credibility.

Now let us review an example of a constructive fraudulent conveyance, one without intent. In a desperate try to save your firm, you decide to sell a large piece of equipment so you can make payroll. You place a classified advertisement in your weekly trade newspaper stating the server is available for the best offer.

From this ad, you get one response. The person offers you $2,500, and you take it gladly. Within two months, you declare bankruptcy and the court's trustee analyzes your transactions over the past two years.

Based on the court's review, they discover the equipment that you sold for $2,500 could have netted $7,500 in an orderly liquidation. This is a constructive fraudulent conveyance.

The person who bought the equipment must return it, and now he has a claim on the estate for $2,500. He will likely only get cents on the dollar on his claim. In this case, you were only doing your job so the Business Judgment Rule covers you, and you do not have to worry about criminal penalties.

More on Personal asset protection

As far as personal asset protection goes, there is good news and there is bad news. First, let's go through the good news. It is possible to protect all your personal assets from creditors.

You do not have to lose anything if you have a personal asset protection plan in place. Such a plan helps prevent angry creditors (and possibly investors) from dragging you into long and involved lawsuits.

Simply put, if you do not have any assets available for a settlement, then the creditors are less likely to sue you. If you have an ironclad protection plan in place, you and your spouse should have peace of mind. You will be able to keep everything for which you have worked so hard.

Now here's the bad news. If you do not already have that plan in place immediately, you have no protection for at least two years.

Under these circumstances, a new personal asset protection plan becomes a fraudulent conveyance. The court will not uphold it.

Why? Because a personal asset protection plans require moving assets from your business to your personal use. You are effectively giving yourself a "gift" much like the son-in-law example in the previous section.

Even without a current plan, you can get an estate planner immediately. The planner may have some tricks up his or her sleeve, and they may already have the foundation for an asset protection plan without even knowing it.

To help you understand this better, the next few sections introduce some topics you should discuss with an estate planner.

Be aware that property only remains exempt if a creditor has not placed a lien on it. For example, many business owners give a personal guarantee pledging their home to the bank if they default on their business loan. This cancels your homestead exemption.

Therefore, try to avoid having liens and guarantees against exempt property. Also, if you already have these liens in place, have them transferred, if possible, to nonexempt assets.

Strategic funding of your business

After protecting the personal assets through exemptions, you must protect your business assets. This is only proper if your business is a separate legal entity (corporation or LLC) and not a sole proprietorship or partnership.

If you have not done so already, you may get some added liability protection by changing from a sole proprietorship or partnership into a separate legal entity. Be aware that this protection is not absolute. Again, consult your estate planner and attorney to see if this makes sense for you.

Strategic funding means reducing the asset base in your business by transferring these assets to another legal entity. The goal is to give creditors and plaintiffs many fewer assets that they can "go after."

You can do this in several ways. First, pay yourself and your spouse if he or she works in the business, a market-based salary. This is a legitimate way to put the firm's cash into your personal bank account.

Second, you can lease or loan to the firm assets that you would normally have donated. Make sure that these leases and loans have the asset held as a security interest. Get your lawyer's help here. You will need to be sure that your claim is "perfected." Perfected means officially recorded. Different types of property such as real estate, vehicles and all other types of personal or business property can be "perfected" through different channels. Make sure you talk to an attorney and protect your assets – properly!

If your business does take bankruptcy, you become one of the firm's secured creditors if your security claim is perfected. Having priority over unsecured creditors, you will likely get back your assets in the bankruptcy proceeding.

Explore this topic with your estate planner thoroughly. This conversation will be especially important if you are making further personal investments in the business to help turn it around. Don't just put your money into the company. Loan the business your money and make sure the loan is written, secured by the assets of the business and perfected.

Trusts & Other Entities

Trusts can be a useful asset protection device. Effectively a trust is a separate legal entity from the person. Therefore, if you place assets into a trust, creditors have a difficult time attaching to them in a settlement.

One good way to use trusts is to set up separate trusts for you and your spouse. You would place the assets at high risk (like your business) in your trust. Your spouse's trust, on the other hand, gets those assets that need protection (like your house.) Then, if a creditor or someone else sues you and your business, your spouse's trust protects your family's wealth.

Other entities that you should explore are operating and holding companies. With these devices, you divide your business into a holding company that owns the assets and operating companies that lease the assets from the holding company. The operating companies deal direct with suppliers and customers.

Therefore, if one of the operating companies gets into trouble and circumstances force it into bankruptcy, the assets held in the holding company are safe. The theory here is the farther removed the assets are from the troubled business, the less likely you are to lose them.

One asset that you must have in your holding company is the lease of your business real estate property. Often, the underpriced lease contract for a prime location is the most valuable asset that a retail business has and a bankruptcy court can sell your lease without needing the landlord's permission. Therefore, have your lease contract in such a way the holding company is the "tenant" and sublets to the operating company.

Insurance

Your final line of defense is liability insurance. Directors & Officers (D&O) coverage, general liability and employee liability coverage.

Even if you are having a cash crunch, you need to continue to make your premium payments.

If you have done your asset planning well, you should be able to lower your coverage. Your asset base now will be much smaller. Therefore, an ironclad asset protection plan should lower your insurance costs.

Personal Guarantees

"What can I do about my personal guarantees?" Let's look at two strategies on how you can relieve yourself of a personal guarantee.

You may be able to renegotiate the agreements that have your personal guarantee and give instead some other comfort or collateral to the other side.

You can pay off the loan that's backed with your personal guarantee. With this strategy, you make any debts that have your guarantee a priority payment at the expense of other creditors. Once you've paid off these debts, you can then choose to liquidate.

Also look into personal guarantee insurance. If not to cover all of it, some or most of it.

Personal guarantees are a sign of the times.

Marriage and family – you and your spouse should:

- Accept you may be spending time away from the family commitments to focus on the business

- Accept there will be stress until the business makes its turnaround

- Accept that the hard work may be for nothing, but the potential payoff is worth it

- Agree on time limits for getting the business fixed

- Agree on the financial limits that you will personally invest in the business
- Agree on a family budget
- Agree to a backup plan

Emotional health

- Learn from every experience
- Understand what went wrong with the business and how to avoid it in the future
- Don't dish out blame for the past. Look forward

Surviving the crisis: How to get through the next 90 days

You have to move with a sense of urgency – especially now – while you are gathering information. It is too early for anyone to take time out. You have limited choices when it comes to stabilizing the business's cash balance.

You must quickly decide the status - quickly

How much time do you have if left to survive – doing nothing? Gather as much information as possible. What's the state of the financial reporting? Can you get good numbers? Profit & Loss (P&L), Balance Sheet (BS), Accounts Receivable (AR), Accounts Payable (AP) reports.

IMPORTANT: You must stop writing checks until you have a base to make decisions from.

Are you on track to survive the next six months without taking any action?

Section 4 - Manage a Crisis

Surviving the crisis: How to get through the next 90 days

You have limited choices when it comes to stabilizing the business's cash balance. Clearly, you do not have time to set up a new sales and marketing strategy. This can take several months.

Therefore, you must cut the expense side of the profit and loss statement. This means that the business is typically going to get smaller, a lot smaller. Most resistance from entrepreneurs involved with turning around a business comes from the realization of how much smaller a business may need to be to get back to profit.

Entrepreneurs are wired to grow the business, which is not the goal of most turnarounds. Growth being the entrepreneurs solution to a business problem is typically what led the entrepreneur to the trouble they're in now. Think about it this way: When you are dealing with rot, rust or failing systems on everything from buildings, cars, motorcycles, furniture and anything you think of, what's the first thing you need to do? Get back to solid material. Get back to a foundation you can add to. Businesses need to change and sometimes that requires getting a lot smaller.

Quickly decide the status

How much time do you have if left to survive? Gather as much information as possible. What's the state of the financial reporting? Can you get good numbers? You must be able to work from current P&L, BS, AR, AP reports. It doesn't matter if the reports are written by hand or by your CPA. What's important is that you have good numbers to work from. You must stop writing checks until you have a base to make decisions from.

Are you on track to survive the next six months without taking any action?

If you can survive the next six months, all the better. Even if you have six months to live, you will want to know your exact cash position and forecast every week. This way, you can make sure that the business stays on track.

With the luxury of time, you can carve out an uninterrupted four weeks to create and start carrying out a comprehensive turnaround plan.

Take control of cash right now!

- You must make it known that only you can approve an expense – ANY EXPENSE

- You must sign every check – EVERY CHECK

- Freeze hiring – NO HIRING

- Gather cash from subsidiaries and dormant bank accounts – LOCATE ALL THE CASH

For your business to survive, you must stop it from bleeding cash. You must restrict all cash outflows immediately!

You should tell everyone in your business that there will be no more spending without your personal authorization. This includes *all* spending including trips, new materials, office supplies and anything else needing business money. Also, it means no capital outlays, even if you previously approved it. You must sign every purchase order.

In addition, starting immediately, you need to tell the CFO or bookkeeper that you will personally sign every check written on the business's bank account. The only exceptions to this will be payroll and trust funds such as payroll taxes or 401k contributions.

Also, you need to tell human resources and management that there is a freeze on hiring.

You now have complete control of your businesses cash. Only approve spending that is necessary to keep the business running. Also, you will only sign checks that the business needs to keep vendors from shutting you off.

Identify hidden cash that may remain in any subsidiary's bank accounts.

These steps should stop the cash bleeding.

This complete stoppage of cash outflow is only a temporary measure and will likely last up to one month. Second point of contention from most entrepreneurs is that they can't stop writing checks. Failure begins right here! I have never asked an entrepreneur to do anything that isn't possible and for the right reasons. Stop writing checks other than payroll until you have a plan that works. During this time, you must create a plan about who you will pay and when you will pay them. This will be part of the forecasting cash process covered in – Forecast Cash.

Keep these controls on approvals and spending until you are no longer in either a crisis or turnaround. They should be in effect for at least several months.

By approving every expense, you will quickly identify your business's unnecessary spending. Furthermore, the cost side of your P&L will improve quickly with the active intervention. You will use this knowledge to help forecast cash in the next step and develop a turnaround budget.

Forecast cash

- Based on AR and AP and all other information start developing a 13 week cash forecast

- Hold a weekly cash forecast meeting

- Update the 13-week cash forecast weekly

- Approve payments for the week

- Review and adjust results against previous week's forecast

- Set payment dates for new invoices
- Develop steps to avoid a cash crisis
- Set weekly pay-out and collections goals and incentives for payables and receivables employees

Never spend more in a week than you have cash available at the end of the previous week.

Simply stated, on Monday, find out your bank account balance, and do not spend more than that during the week.

How to create the cash forecast

Creating your cash forecast should be a group exercise. It should be a weekly, two-hour meeting if needed to forecast your cash and approve payments.

You should invite the CFO, bookkeeper, the payroll person, the payables person, the receivables person and the top sales person or manager to this meeting. Of course, they should attend every meeting. Each individual contributes a key data point to the cash forecast, and you should hold each person accountable for his or her numbers.

This meeting has several purposes. First, you use it to create the forecast itself. Second, you and your team will decide payments for the week. Third, the meeting will help you find out why the previous week's numbers were not accurate. Fourth, your team will help decide payment dates for each invoice received. Fifth, they will help come up with action steps to avoid a cash crisis.

You need to coach them through these meetings. Here is how you should run the meeting:

- Review their results versus the forecast from the previous week. Find out why they did not receive money expected or why more was spent than sanctioned. This drives accountability and accuracy into the process.

- Update the cash forecast with the latest bank account balance from the previous week, and add another week to the remaining 12 weeks. You are doing a new

13-week forecast starting with the current week.

- Get payroll estimates from the payroll person for the next 13 weeks including all costs like payroll taxes.

- Review all invoices and decide who you must absolutely pay this week. Then decide when to pay new invoices that they have received in the past week.

- Have a discussion and decide how to include payments into their forecast for invoices that they have not received yet. Likely these numbers will be close to their current payments.

- Get an estimate for collections from the receivables person. If he or she is on top of collection calls and accounts, the receivables person should be accurate in this estimate for the next two to three weeks. For the out-periods, it depends on the sales level and collection history. The sales manager should be able to give you an accurate estimate for these weekly sales and collections.

Find cost savings

- Start going through a P&L in detail - line-by-line

- Cut everything you don't need. Be tough!

Restructure the trade debt

Start by building a clear picture of any leases, supplier debt, reliance's, relationships. Gather the detail.

Layoff deadwood and underperformers

Look for underperforming employees and underperforming departments.

You should also look at removing and restructuring overpaid managers and staff now.

Because of the time constraints that you face, you cannot do this with a well-thought out plan. Just use shared intuition and make the cuts. Cut more than you need to. Sounds harsh! If you undercut you expose yourself to continued risk. Overcut employees can always be hired back without adding to the exposure.

Collect money from your customers

- Set a goal: collect something from every invoice

- Call your delinquent customers 2 or 3 times weekly

- Call your counterpart

- Get a collection agency involved with seriously delinquent accounts

- Consider suing the delinquent customer

- Invoice the customers as quickly as you can

- Do not allow salespeople to give extended terms unless it is a competitive requirement

- Give terms that will get you paid quicker like 2/10 (that is 2% off the invoice if paid within 10 days of receipt)

- Call your customers a few days before the invoice due date with a friendly reminder

Sell the receivables to a factoring company

There are good and bad factoring companies. A factoring company will purchase your accounts receivable (commercial accounts) for up to 85% of the invoice amount up front when the invoice is signed depending on a number of "factors" such as the credit worthiness of the customer. The factoring company is absorbing the risk of getting paid. The remaining 15% is paid typically when the factoring company collects payment from the customer in full. This frees up your immediate cash flow based on the invoices in hand. Factoring used to be a really expensive and even troublesome method of financing a business. Factoring companies acted more like debt collectors with your customers and more like loan sharks with entrepreneurs.

While some still exist, many have moved on to become an everyday part of small business financing. Do your homework and again look for references from people that count – people like you. If you can't get references move on to someone else! Factoring costs vary greatly so make sure you know the Annualized Percentage Rate (APR) of the financed amount.

Start restructuring the long-term agreements

Long term agreements may be acting like a noose around your businesses neck. Every agreement needs to be looked at. No matter what the holder of the agreement threatens you need to look at what's good or bad for the business. Check with your attorney about bankruptcy effects on long-term contracts. The premise being that you should know and be able to share with the contract holder what bankruptcy would mean for their contract.

If there is a way where the contract holder can benefit from negotiating verses bankruptcy the option needs to be offered. A calculation can be performed to show that if bankruptcy was taken that the contract holder would receive X pennies per dollar. Let's say that under bankruptcy the contract holder is shown to get back 15 cents per dollar currently owed under contract value. Therefore if the contract holder was to accept 30 cents per dollar they would be better off by negotiating the end of the existing contract or negotiating a new contract if the business is still important to them. This helps your cash flow and if the same strategy is used on debt and payable negotiations, it helps reduce your debt too.

Start restructuring long-term bank debt

When it comes to restructuring your bank debt you are better off allowing a capable business attorney or debt negotiator handle it. It is going to be very difficult for you the person that is responsible for the debt to negotiate directly with the lender when you have personal guarantees attached. The bank knows it will win that emotional battle with you. If you can't get past the emotional battle there is no getting to negotiate terms.

Sell unproductive assets

Don't keep an asset that doesn't generate a return on investment. Take a good look around. Clean up and cash out! If you have something sitting there that isn't contributing to the sales of your business get it sold.

Look at sales and leaseback

If you own the real estate that the business operates in, should you sell it and lease it back? Real estate was the number one – go-to standard wealth builder for years. I've no doubt it will be again. So the question is really, should you sell your real estate in order to reinvest into the business? The only reason to invest in the business is if you are confident that the problems have been addressed and that you will get a return on the investment. Don't make the mistake of just throwing good money after lost money in the hope that something's going to change. It's not going to change just because you want it to.

Section 5 - Get Back By Design

The business isn't going to get fixed overnight. You have to break your own bad habits before you can change others habits. Remember it typically takes 90 days to get control over a struggling small business – at a minimum!

Take control of the cash first. That's the blood of the business. To take control you need to stop all cash from leaving the business. "I can't do that..." BS! You can do that. You will be amazed what you can do when you take on the survivor attitude. I am expecting you to push yourself past your own limitations. There is nothing in here that I'm expecting of you that hasn't already been done by millions of entrepreneurs and managers. Don't try to address everything all at once. You need to plan and prioritize. You don't have to be perfect, you have to be a survivor.

Once you are able to take control of the cash you need to manage the process of identifying and changing problem areas. That does not happen overnight so don't set yourself up to fail.

Accelerating the solution, do you need more help?

If you've been following the solutions to this point and you're somewhere between thirty to sixty days into your turnaround you should have been able to buy yourself the time needed to make the right choices. You should be cash flow positive, meaning you are no longer losing money. If you are cash flow positive you have bought yourself the time and the room to build things the right way.

This does not mean you are ready to start hiring back or releasing the restrictions already imposed.

The first goal was to stop you from bleeding. If you're not bleeding we can move you from life support to critical care. From critical care you eventually move to a stable condition...

Decide if you need any of the following to help lift the weight off your shoulders:

- Coach

- Turnaround Specialist
- New outside accountant
- New attorney

For each expert that you need, do the following

- Create a list of at least three prospects for each category
- Interview each one thoroughly
- Check their references
- Select the expert you feel confident with
- Don't hire a yes man/woman

Creating a Winning Turnaround Plan

Act like a turnaround leader

- Take on the characteristics of a survivor
- Put aside your preconceived notions about what will work and won't work

- Look into everything and everyone
- Fire the people that become obstacles in your path. There is no room for nonbelievers

Gather information

- Delegate daily tasks, free up your time to gather information and create a plan
- Meet with the senior team and employees to tell them about your mission
- Talk to employees
- Identify and interview the "quiet" employee
- Identify the "troublemakers"
- Evaluate everyone's "fit" within the new organization
- Talk to third parties about what they want to see change in your business
- Interview your top 5 customers

- Interview former customers that have recently dropped the business
- Interview top 5 vendors
- Review sales and marketing information
- Decide which market segments give you the most business
- Decide what salespeople are contributing most to your top and bottom line
- Ask yourself, "Is the sales plan real?"
- Review financial information
- Ask these questions:
- What's causing trends in your financial statements?
- Where are you spending your money?
- Do the financial statements make sense?
- How much debt leverage do you have?
- How long is it taking to pay suppliers?

- How long does it take to collect your receivables?
- What is the actual profitability by customer, product or service?
- Get a new physical count of your inventory that can be trusted
- Write off old and excess inventory
- Identify inventory minimums
- Identify inventory maximums
- Identify ways to increase your number of inventory turns

Analyze the data and create your turnaround strategies

- Identify your core business
- Select your product and services mix
- Decide your competitive positioning
- Develop your sales forecast and sales strategy

- Redesign your organization and reduce headcount
- Find cost savings
- Create operational plans
- Develop a funding strategy
- Create financial projections

Build a new management team

- Fire, or reassign anyone that's no longer on the team

Hold an alignment meeting with new management team

- Secure a meeting location for an off-site meeting
- Make sure everyone leaves the meeting in complete agreement on the business's direction, turnaround strategies and action items
- Fire anyone who tries to sabotage the meeting or the plan

Write the final turnaround plan and create an action plan

- Consider writing different versions of the turnaround plan for different audiences such as employees, bankers, creditors

- Consider subcontracting to a full-time turnaround manager or part time coach if you are struggling with the turnaround of your business

Rethinking the organizational structure for success

- Consider outsourcing

- Put in place a flat organizational structure

- Encourage generation of new, money saving and profit making ideas

- Encourage communication of bad news without retaliation

- Consider using committees, task forces and project teams instead of adding new departments and divisions to their organization structure

Use the "quick" method for designing your structure

- Decide on a flat organization chart

- Cut out departments, divisions, and people that do not fit with your new direction

- Reorganize the work if necessary to meet the needs of the turnaround plan

- Force fit the design to two or three layers of management for small to medium size businesses

- Downsize the business

- Bring the organization up to speed on the new organizational structure

- Put in place measurable goals and objectives for each department and manager and even employee

Use budgets

- To set expense and sales goals
- To communicate the turnaround plan
- As a training tool

Having a successful interaction with your banker

- Share your turnaround plan
- Back up your actions based on data and results
- Give time period to complete execution of the plan
- Share financial projections
- Show how you will repay the loan
- Share when and how much you can pay
- Let them know how they can help you
- Ask what other information they need from you

- Schedule monthly meetings
- Share progress on your turnaround in future meetings
- Consider using pre-bankruptcy technique to get some type of immediate relief or consideration
- Get help from an attorney if the bank calls the loan

The layoff

Decide on a severance package

- Consider a waiver limiting the right to sue as a consideration for a severance package
- Do not reject unemployment insurance claims

Select a date and time for the layoff

- Do all layoffs on the same day
- Have security personnel ready

Schedule a same day meeting for all remaining employees immediately after the last lay off.

Don't leave the remaining employees hanging. It is important to let them know you are taking these steps to safeguard the business and their futures.

- Have final paychecks ready!

Run the termination meeting professionally

- Call the employee into the meeting as privately as possible

- Tell the employee that you are laying him or her off

- Go through the termination letter with emphasis on the severance package

- Discuss top-line points of the waiver, if this is a condition for receiving the severance

- Give the date by which employee must sign the waiver in return for the severance and tell the employee that he or she is welcome to have an attorney review it

- Discuss employees' COBRA rights and go over any other forms such as pension and savings plan forms in the communication package

- Go over the pre-written reference letter (if given)

- Ask if employee has any questions about the layoff, the severance package, the waiver...

- Discuss the return of property belonging to the business such as laptops, credit cards, cell phones, and business cars

- Communicate how you will manage telephone calls, emails and mail

- Discuss immediate next steps. (These may include how the employee will leave his, or her, workspace and that the employee should leave the building immediately)

- Give the employee the final paycheck and say thank you for his or her contributions to the business

- Adjourn the meeting

- Document what you and the employee said in the termination meeting and note any agreements

Hold the Remaining Employee meeting

- Redirect strong emotions to turning around the business

- Recognize the loss of good employees in the layoff

- Give the business reasons for the layoff

- Take sole responsibility for the business's downturn and the layoffs

- Tell them you are heartbroken as well

- Open the floor to questions and take the blame for everything

- Do not blame a fired employee for any of the business's troubles
- Present your turnaround plan
- Explain the new organizational design
- Explain why everyone needs to be cost conscious
- Ask for more questions
- Let everyone go home early

How to motivate the remaining employees during the turnaround

- Admit past mistakes
- Ask questions to find out morale
- Always be energetic and upbeat
- Come in first every day, be the last to leave
- Communicate good news regardless how trivial

How To Save A Small Business

- Convince the team that a turnaround is probable
- Create a procedure for employees to suggest improvements
- Empower your employees
- Ensure job security of valuable employees
- Get to know everyone personally
- Give job titles
- Give time off for a job well done
- Have an open-door policy
- Set up bonus compensation
- Incentives for beating goals
- Live with the rank-and-file for a day
- Make having fun a mandate
- Name an employee of the month

- Recognize employee contributions publicly
- Set an example

Reducing your debt!

Do-it-yourself debt restructuring

- Send creditors a letter to calm them
- Meet with the IRS and other taxing authorities
- Decide strategic versus nonstrategic vendors
- Plan your debt-restructuring offer
- Contact strategic suppliers
- Contact nonstrategic suppliers
- Communicate monthly with creditors
- Set up a procedure to handle creditor calls

Debt restructuring – Using a professional

Consider a debt management business to save yourself time and money. A professional debt negotiator should be compensated by a percentage of the money saved! The more they save you, the more they make. Don't pay upfront or other fees that take away from their motivation of saving you money.

Ways to find more money fast

- Expense cuts
- Revenue growth
- Asset sales
- Receivables management
- Debt and vendor management

Stay and Grow or Sell

You are probably between twelve and eighteen months into your turnaround and things are starting to go well. Now what? Well that's up to you. You could stay and continue to manage the business in the way you've learned how. Yes, it's hard work – every day. But you've figured it out now. You could spend the next five years working to make more money than you did in the last ten years if you really get things right.

You could attempt to sell the business but it's too close to the negative period to see any real value being added to the business. Is it more valuable? Sure, but it's going to take three years of proving profits to get someone to pay you for "your design to profitability".

Celebrate your turnaround success

- Have a party
- Announce the turnaround is officially over
- Hand out awards

Conclusion

So on reflection of everything you are about to go through or everything you've been through, turning around a small business is a complicated but possible task. So many businesses are in trouble because they get lost somewhere along the way. We all know that within every industry there are those that are winning and those that are losing.

We have the ability to become one of the businesses that are winning.

It takes guts and a lot of hard work to turn a business around. The odds are against you and so are most of the people you talk to during the process. Decide whether you want to be a survivor or a victim of circumstance. It's going to be the easiest decision you'll get to make.

Notes

Notes

Notes

Notes

Notes

Notes

www.ingramcontent.com/pod-product-compliance
Lightning Source LLC
Chambersburg PA
CBHW071801200526
45167CB00017B/935